XTREME CARS

LAMBORGHINI

A&D Xtreme
BOLD HI-LO NONFICTION
An imprint of Abdo Publishing
abdobooks.com

S.L. HAMILTON

TAKE IT TO THE XTREME!

GET READY FOR AN XTREME ADVENTURE! THE PAGES OF THIS BOOK WILL TAKE YOU INTO THE THRILLING WORLD OF LAMBORGHINIS. WHEN YOU HAVE FINISHED READING THIS BOOK, TAKE THE XTREME CHALLENGE ON PAGE 45 ABOUT WHAT YOU'VE LEARNED!

ABDOBOOKS.COM

Published by Abdo Publishing, a division of ABDO, PO Box 398166, Minneapolis, Minnesota 55439.

052022
092022

THIS BOOK CONTAINS RECYCLED MATERIALS

Editor: John Hamilton

Copy Editor: Tamara L. Britton

Graphic Design: Sue Hamilton

Cover Design: Laura Graphenteen

Cover Photo: Shutterstock

Interior Photos & Illustrations: All photos Automobili Lamborghini S.p.A., except: Shutterstock-pgs 9 (bottom right inset), 13 (bottom inset) & 14-15 (bottom).

LIBRARY OF CONGRESS CONTROL NUMBER: 2021942763

PUBLISHER'S CATALOGING-IN-PUBLICATION DATA

Names: Hamilton, S.L., author.

Title: Lamborghini / by S.L. Hamilton

Description: Minneapolis, Minnesota : Abdo Publishing, 2023 | Series: Xtreme cars | Includes online resources and index.

Identifiers: ISBN 9781532196072 (lib. bdg.) | ISBN 9781098217006 (ebook)

Subjects: LCSH: Lamborghini automobile--Juvenile literature. | Sports cars--Juvenile literature. | Cars (Automobiles)--Juvenile literature.

Classification: DDC 629.2221--dc23

TABLE OF CONTENTS

CHAPTER 1

LAMBORGHINI SPORTS CARS

Lamborghinis are a symbol of power, wealth, and **luxury**. These Italian sports cars race down the world's roads in a blur of color. Lambos are known for their cutting-edge design and **aerodynamic** engineering.

XTREME FACT

The Lamborghini design was originally created by Filippo Perini, who got his inspiration from fighter planes.

Lamborghini Aventador

CHAPTER 2

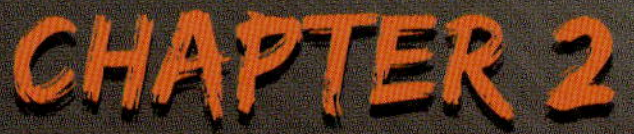

LAMBORGHINI'S HISTORY

Ferruccio Lamborghini was a successful inventor and businessman in Italy in the mid-1900s. He owned cars made by Alfa Romeo, Jaguar, Maserati, and Ferrari. Lamborghini felt he could create a faster and better road car. In 1963, he founded Automobili Ferruccio Lamborghini.

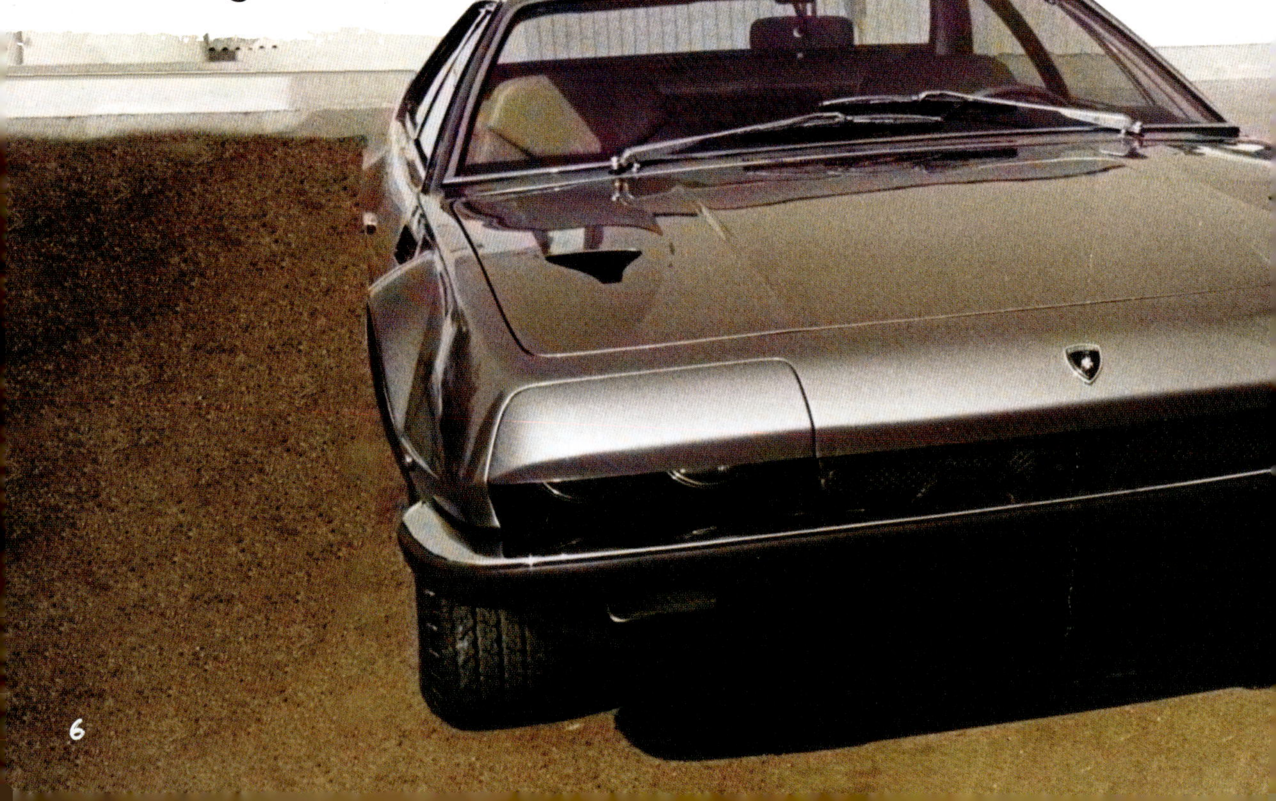

XTREME FACT

The first Lamborghinis were tractors. Ferruccio worked on tractor engines on his family's farm. He started his own tractor business in 1947. Lamborghini tractors are still built today.

Ferruccio Lamborghini

The Lamborghini **logo** is a bull in a shield. Born on April 28, 1916, Ferruccio's zodiac sign was Taurus the bull. The logo also showed his interest in bullfighting. Bulls represented power, speed, and danger. Nearly all of his cars were named after famous fighting bulls, bullfighters, or their weapons.

The first Lamborghini 350 GT was presented to Ferruccio. It had the bull logo and his signature on the front hood.

The company uses a stylized text often seen on the back of their vehicles.

Lamborghini's early logo (left) had a golden fighting bull. The modern bull looks fiercer.

CHAPTER 3

THE EARLY YEARS OF LAMBORGHINI

The 350 GT was Lamborghini's first **production car**, built from 1963-1966. It was lightweight and powerful, with a V12 engine designed to send the 2-seater sports car to a top speed of 158 mph (255 kph).

From the 350 GT on, every production Lamborghini has had high-performance Pirelli tires.

LAMBORGHINI GT SPECIFICATIONS

YEARS PRODUCED
1963-1968

MAXIMUM HORSEPOWER
320 (400 GT model)

ZERO TO 60 MPH (97 KPH)
5.8 seconds (400 GT model)

The 400 GT's redesigned larger body allowed for a back seat.

The 400 GT followed from 1966-1968. This **grand tourer** was roomier with a 2+2 passenger design (2 people in front and 2 in back). It was still powerful, reaching a top speed of 168 mph (270 kph).

The Lamborghini Miura (myur-uh) was the fastest **production car** in the world when it was introduced in 1966. It had a top speed of 174 mph (280 kph). The mid-engine, 2-seater raced from 0-60 mph (97 kph) in 6.7 seconds.

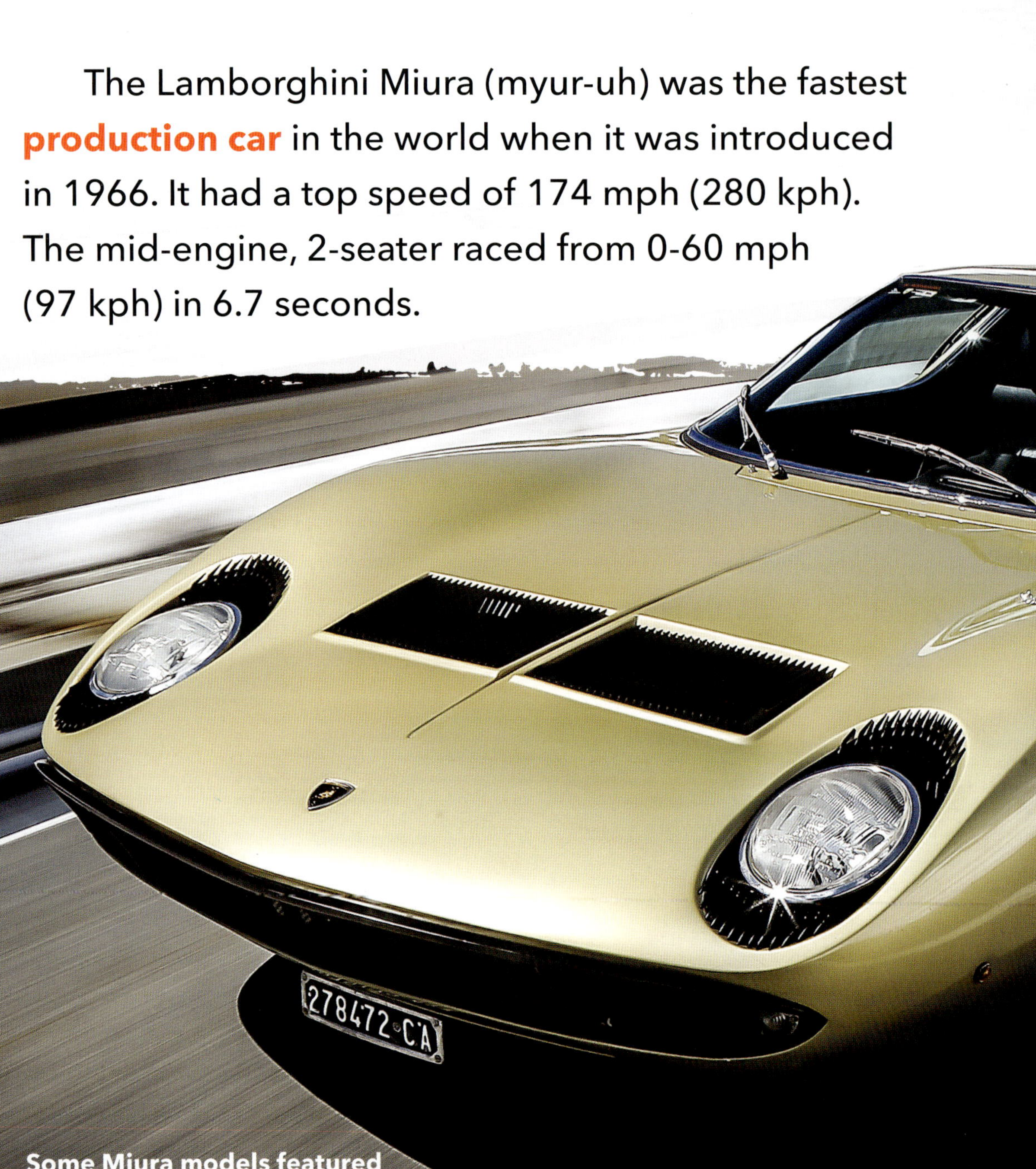

Some Miura models featured retractable headlights with "eyelashes" built into the design.

The Miura was named after fierce fighting bulls from Spain.

The Islero replaced Lamborghini's 400 GT. Built from 1968-1969, the V12 **grand tourer** was named after a powerful bull that killed a matador. The 2+2 **coupe** had a top speed of 154 mph (248 kph).

The Espada was Lambo's second new car introduction of 1968. Like the Islero, it was a 2+2 V12 coupe, but its design was more daring. Various Espada models were built until 1978, but the car's body changed little. Its top speed reached 155 mph (250 kph).

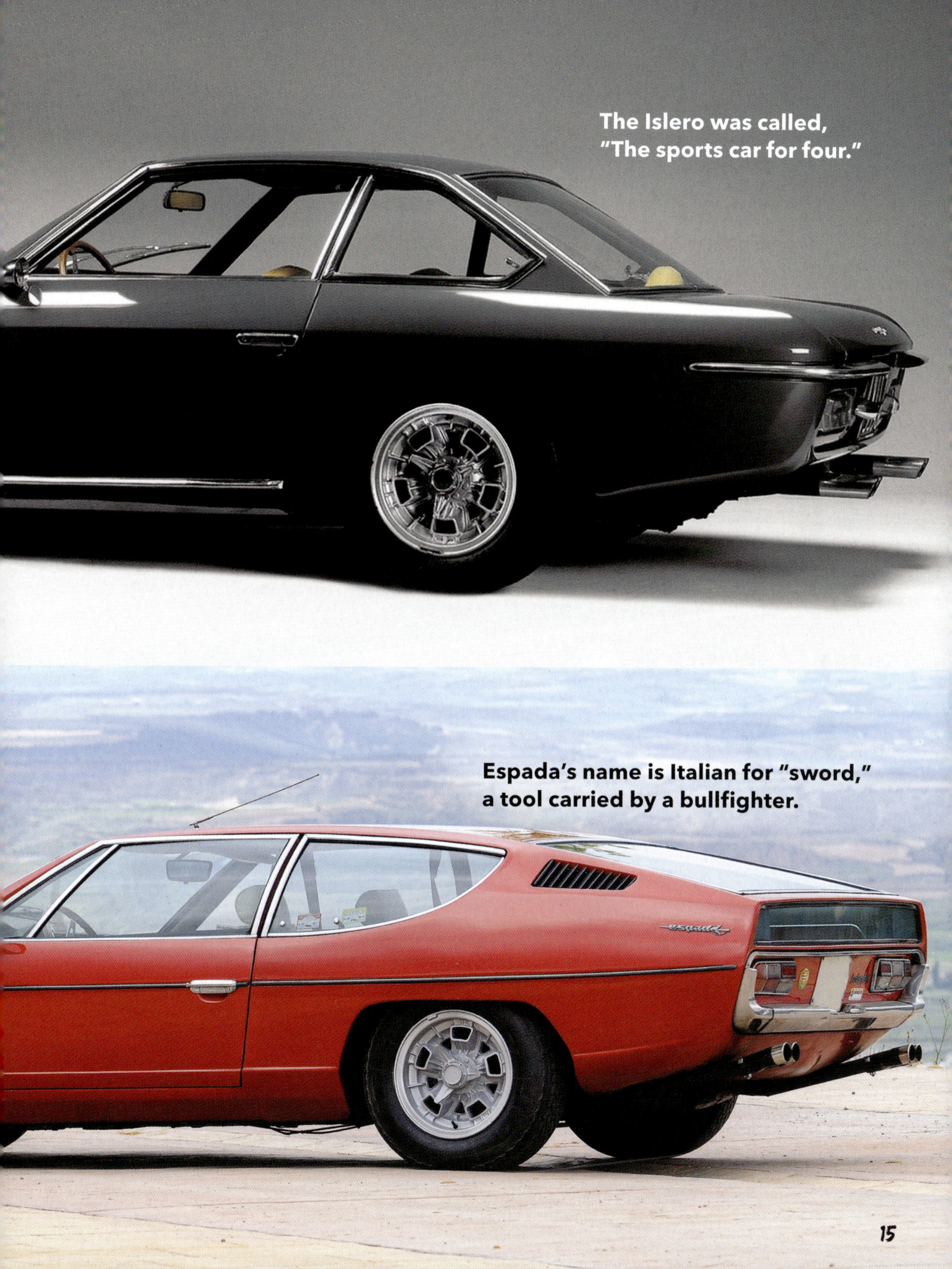

The Islero was called, "The sports car for four."

Espada's name is Italian for "sword," a tool carried by a bullfighter.

CHAPTER 4

LAMBORGHINI CHANGES IN THE 1970s

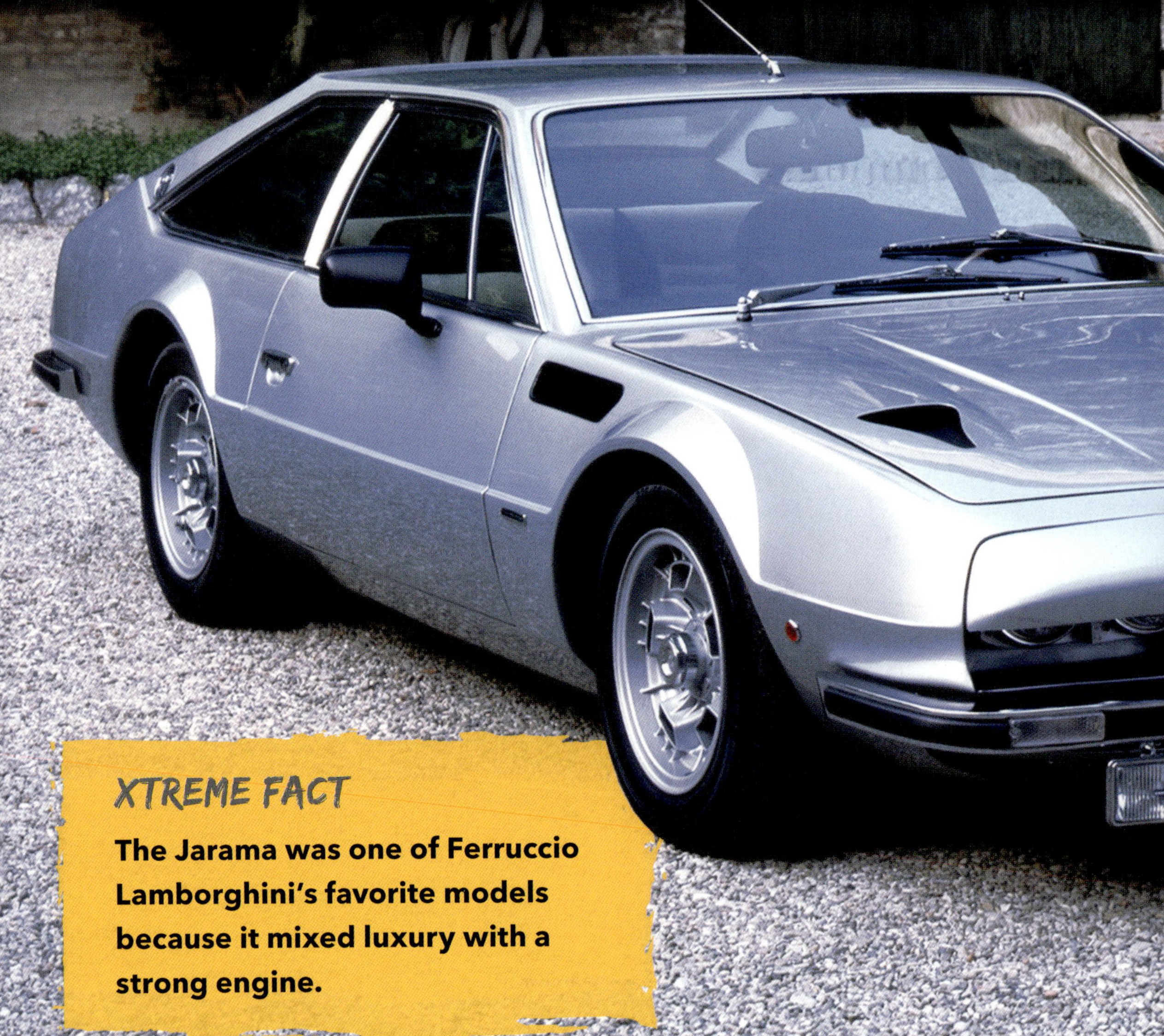

XTREME FACT

The Jarama was one of Ferruccio Lamborghini's favorite models because it mixed luxury with a strong engine.

JARAMA SPECIFICATIONS

YEARS PRODUCED
1970-1976

MAXIMUM HORSEPOWER
352 (Jarama 400 GT)

ZERO TO 60 MPH (97 KPH)
7 seconds (Jarama 400 GT)

Jarama was named after bulls from Spain's Jarama River area.

In 1970, the Jarama 2+2 **coupe** came out. It replaced the Islero and met United States auto standards. The front-engine **grand tourer** had a shorter **chassis** and a heavy body. Its top speed was 155 mph (250 kph).

The world faced an oil crisis in the early 1970s. Gas-guzzling sports cars had terrible sales. Lamborghini's response was to develop smaller V8 sports cars. The Urraco was introduced in 1972. Its name meant "little bull." It still reached a top speed of 155 mph (250 kph).

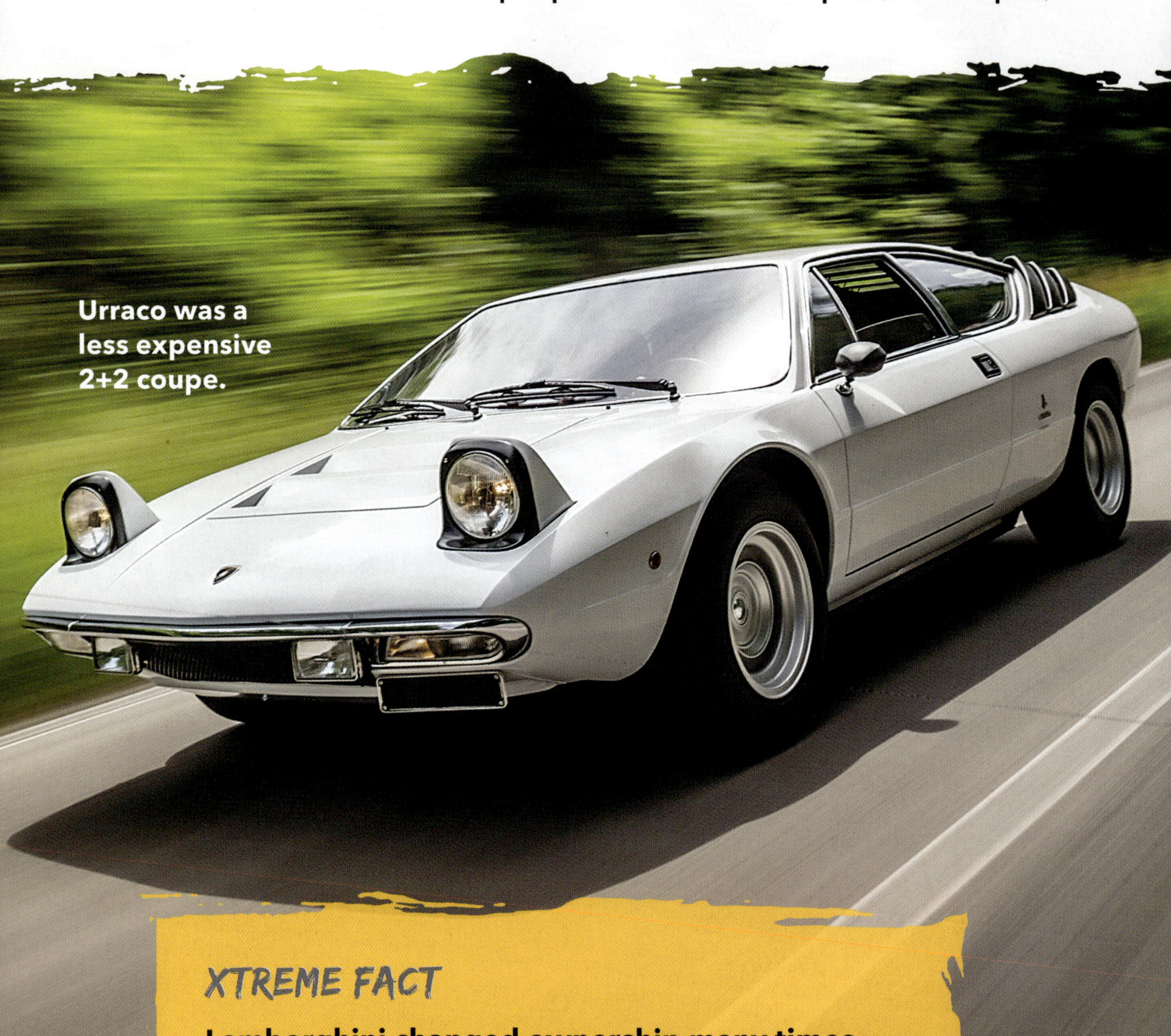

Urraco was a less expensive 2+2 coupe.

XTREME FACT

Lamborghini changed ownership many times. The company nearly went bankrupt until America's Chrysler Corporation purchased it in 1987.

The Silhouette replaced the Urraco in 1976. It featured a detachable **targa roof** that helped the car compete with American convertibles. The V8s were fast, sporty, and less expensive. However, the company was in trouble. Ferruccio sold Lamborghini in 1972 and retired in 1974.

The Silhouette had a top speed of 162 mph (260 kph).

The Lamborghini Countach (coon-tash) became one of the company's most successful cars of all time. Built from 1974-1990, the sleek supercar featured scissor doors, sky-facing side windows, and louvered side vents that cooled the powerful V12 engine. The first Countach LP400 model went from 0-60 mph (0-97 kph) in 5.6 seconds.

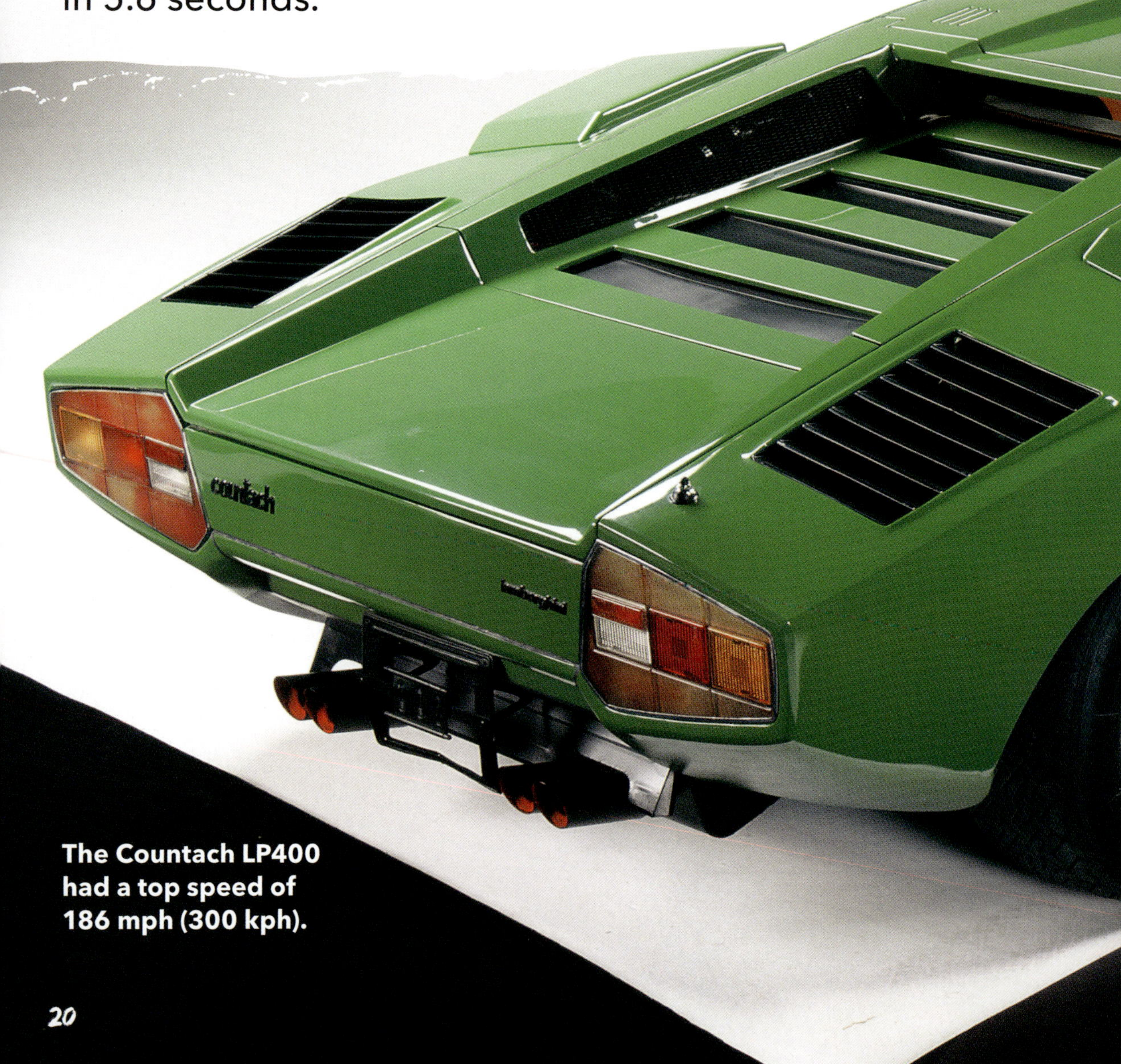

The Countach LP400 had a top speed of 186 mph (300 kph).

XTREME FACT

Countach's name is not a type of bull. It's a slang term for "amazing beauty" in the Piedmontese language of northwestern Italy.

Scissor doors, which swivel up, are also called Lambo doors.

CHAPTER 5

LAMBORGHINI IN THE 1980s & 1990s

In the early 1980s, the Countach's winning design continued to support the company. The new Jalpa replaced the Silhouette in 1981. Jalpa was Lambo's last V8 engine sedan. Although sporty, with a **targa roof** and a top speed of 154 mph (248 kph), it was designed for comfortable driving.

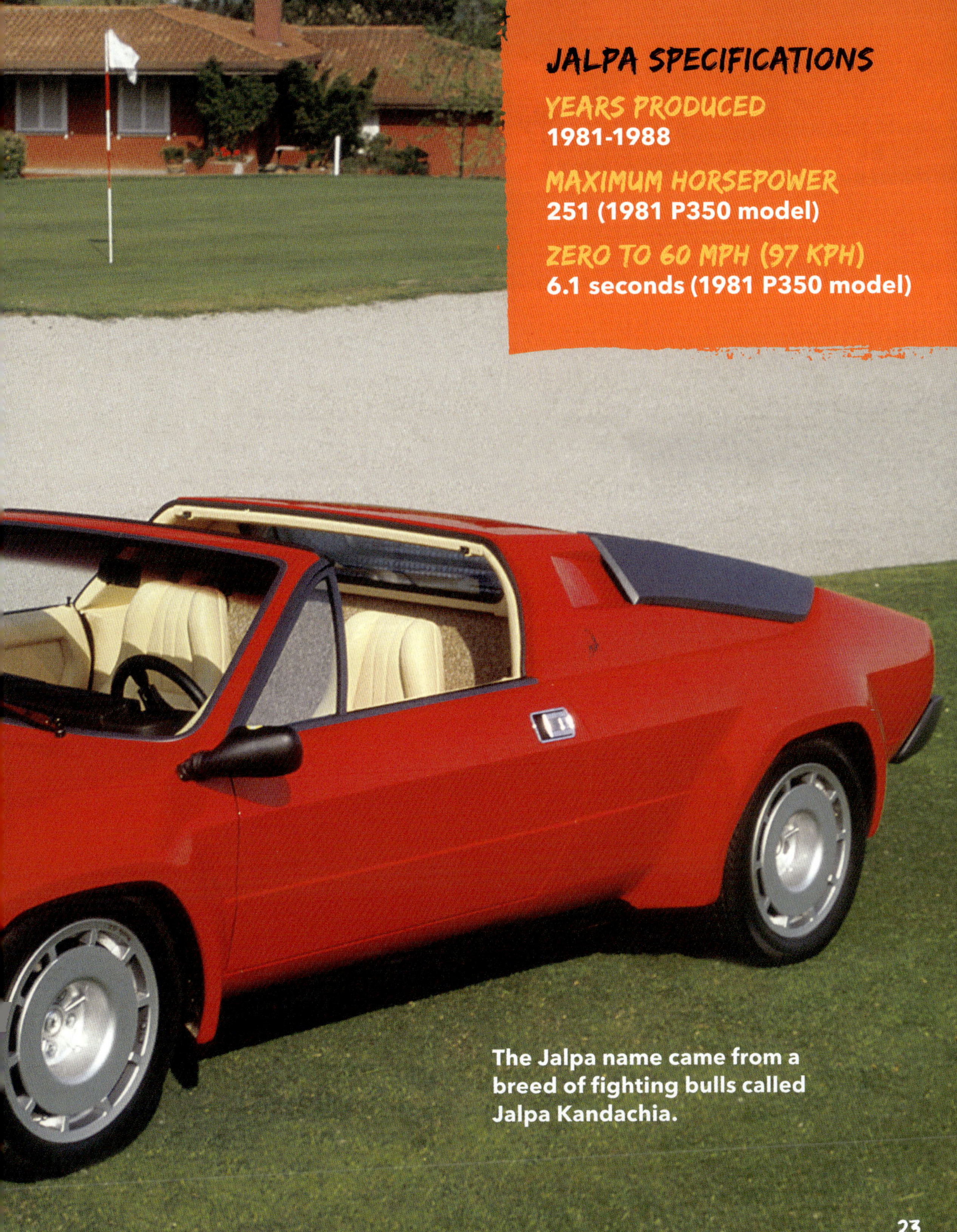

JALPA SPECIFICATIONS

YEARS PRODUCED
1981-1988

MAXIMUM HORSEPOWER
251 (1981 P350 model)

ZERO TO 60 MPH (97 KPH)
6.1 seconds (1981 P350 model)

The Jalpa name came from a breed of fighting bulls called Jalpa Kandachia.

Diablo's name comes from a legendary fierce bull from the 1800s. Diablo means "devil" in Spanish.

The Chrysler Corporation purchased Lamborghini in 1987. Their first Lambo introduction was the Diablo in 1990. It replaced the Countach. The Michigan company's design team smoothed the car's body, losing its sharp lines.

The Diablo featured a sound system, air conditioning, and adjustable seats and steering wheel for the driver's comfort. It boasted a top speed of 202 mph (325 kph) and could go 0-60 mph (0-97 kph) in 4.5 seconds.

CHAPTER 6

LAMBORGHINI IN THE 2000s

In 1998, Lamborghini was purchased by Germany's Volkswagen Group. They introduced the Murciélago (mur-see-ah-lago) in 2001. Its V12 engine mixed with a light **carbon fiber** body and low-to-the-ground styling made it *superveloce* (high speed). It reached 213 mph (342 kph).

The top of the Murciélago is only 4 feet (1.2 m) off the ground.

MURCIÉLAGO SPECIFICATIONS

YEARS PRODUCED
2001-2010

MAXIMUM HORSEPOWER
572 (2001 model)

ZERO TO 60 MPH (97 KPH)
3.6 seconds (2001 model)

Murciélago was named after a famous bull that survived a bullfight in 1879. The name means "bat" in Spanish.

Gallardo's name came from a Spanish bullfighting breed from the 1700s.

The Gallardo (guy-are-doe) was built from 2003-2013. It became one of Lamborghini's best-selling vehicles. Lambo called it "a sports car for day-to-day driving."

XTREME FACT

A few Lamborghini Gallardos were modified and used by police departments in Italy, England, and Panama.

The first Gallardo LP560 had a V10 engine and a top speed of 192 mph (309 kph). **Coupes**, convertibles, and *superleggera* (super lightweight) models were made.

CHAPTER 7

MODERN LAMBORGHINIS PUSH THE LIMITS

The Aventador was introduced in 2011 and new models continued to 2022. Its V12 engine offers blistering acceleration, sending the **hypercar** from zero to a top speed of 221 mph (355 kph) in seconds. The car's shrieking power is loved by its drivers.

AVENTADOR SPECIFICATIONS

YEARS PRODUCED
2011-2022

MAXIMUM HORSEPOWER
769 (LP 780-4 Ultimae)

ZERO TO 60 MPH (97 KPH)
2.8 seconds (LP 780-4 Ultimae)

Aventador's name comes from an award-winning bull that entered the bullfighting ring in 1993.

Removable roof panels are stored in the front luggage compartment of the Aventador roadster.

The Aventador roadster model was introduced in 2012, a year after the **coupe**. It includes an attachable wind deflector to help with interior airflow at its high speed of up to 218 mph (351 kph).

Lambo's Huracán was introduced in 2014 with thrilling **aerodynamic** lines designed to cut through the air. It features superbright **LED lighting** throughout the vehicle.

The Huracán **coupe's** V10 engine takes it from 0-60 mph (97 kph) in 3.2 seconds. The supercar has a top speed of 202 mph (325 kph).

Huracán is Spanish for "hurricane," but the name comes from a courageous fighting bull from 1879.

LAMBORGHINI
HURACÁN
EVO

Inside the two-person Huracán is an 8.4-inch (21-cm) touchscreen to control the car's functions and entertainment systems. Leather, **Alcantara**, or **Carbon Skin** seats finish the beautiful Italian-designed interior.

An original Countach (top) races next to a modern Countach LPI 800-4.

Lamborghini created a limited edition Countach LPI 800-4 to celebrate the famous car's 50th anniversary. The **hypercar** maintains the classic model's lines, but with an updated look. The powerful V12 engine gives a top speed of 221 mph (355 kph).

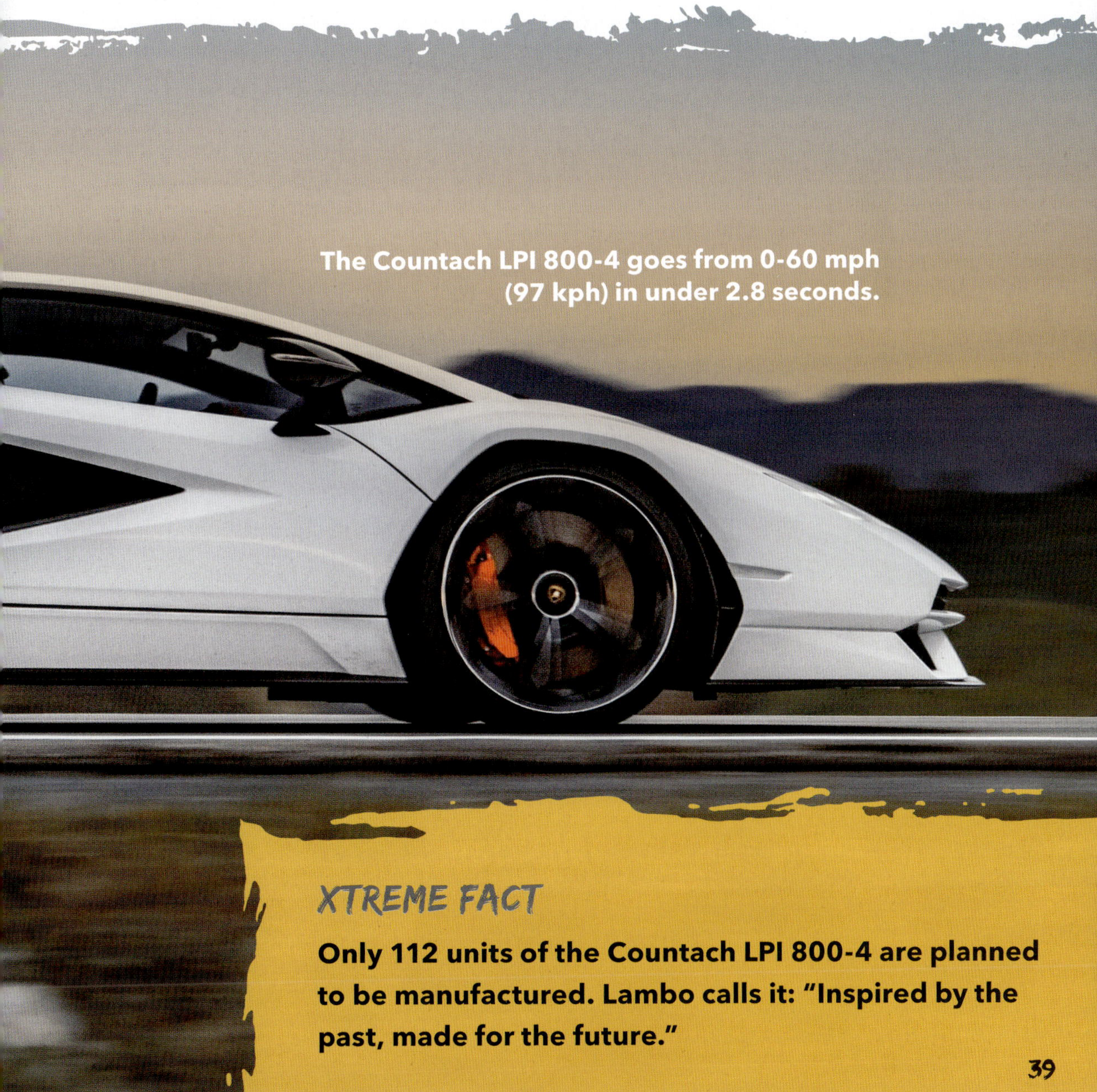

The Countach LPI 800-4 goes from 0-60 mph (97 kph) in under 2.8 seconds.

XTREME FACT

Only 112 units of the Countach LPI 800-4 are planned to be manufactured. Lambo calls it: "Inspired by the past, made for the future."

LAMBORGHINI RACE CARS

Lamborghini's racing vehicles are produced by their Squadra Corse (Team Racing) division. The Huracán Super Trofeo EVO2 model is made for **grand touring** (GT) racers. It's designed to win with a V10 engine, 9-position traction control, and **carbon fiber** body.

HURACÁN SUPER TROFEO EVO2 SPECIFICATIONS

YEARS PRODUCED
2014-Present

MAXIMUM HORSEPOWER
620 (2022 model)

ZERO TO 60 MPH (97 KPH)
2.9 seconds (2022 model)

The Huracán Super Trofeo EVO2 has a top speed of 174 mph (280 kph).

Lamborghini Squadra Corse's SC20 is a one-off roadster. This means each open-top, track car is custom built for a specific driver. The V12 engine has 760 hp and a top speed of more than 200 mph (322 kph).

The SC20 has no roof and no windows. It is street legal.

The SC20's body is made of **carbon fiber**. Airflow over the **aerodynamic** design gives both excellent performance and keeps the driver and passenger comfortable in high-speed, open-cockpit driving.

CHAPTER 9

THE FUTURE

Lamborghini's future includes the introduction of hybrid technology. The Sián FKP 37 is Lambo's first supercar that combines a powerful V12 engine with an electric boost. Beautiful, **aerodynamic** shapes mix with modern engineering to create a Lamborghini that blazes into the 21st century.

Sián (which means "flash of lightning") reaches a top speed of more than 217 mph (350 kph).

XTREME CHALLENGE

TAKE THE QUIZ BELOW AND
PUT WHAT YOU'VE LEARNED TO THE TEST!

1) Who started the Lamborghini company? In what country?

2) What animal is used in the Lamborghini logo? Why was it chosen?

3) What was the first Lambo car? What year was it built?

4) Some Lamborghinis have 2+2 seating. What does that mean?

5) What Lambo car was the "fastest production car in the world" when it was introduced in 1966? What was its top speed?

6) Built from 1974-1990, what Lambo car is considered one of the company's most successful cars of all time?

7) What is Lamborghini's first car to use hybrid technology?

GLOSSARY

aerodynamic – Something that has a shape that reduces the drag, or resistance, of air moving across its surface. Cars with aerodynamic shapes can go faster because they don't have to push as hard to get through the air.

Alcantara – A brand name for a type of soft, microfiber-like material known for its durability. It is used in car interiors in place of leather or vinyl.

carbon fiber – A very strong, thin, and lightweight fiber made of carbon atoms. It may be used in the bodies of cars, planes, and boats.

Carbon Skin – A lightweight fabric made of carbon fiber and epoxy (glue) used in Lamborghinis. It weighs less than leather or Alcantara and helps reduce a sports car's weight.

chassis – The body or frame of a vehicle.

coupe – A passenger car with a fixed roof that cannot be removed, usually with two or three doors. Coupes have a sportier look than four-door sedans, with a sloping rear roofline.

grand tourer (GT) – Cars that can be driven on public roads. GT cars are designed for both performance and comfort.

hypercar – A vehicle whose acceleration and speed are above all other cars.

LED lighting – A type of lighting that is bright and energy efficient. LED stands for light emitting diode.

logo – A graphic symbol that identifies a company.

luxury – Something that adds pleasure or comfort, and is often expensive.

production car – A model of car that is produced by a company that all look the same and are sold to the public.

roadster – A car with an open roof that seats two people.

targa roof – A removable, hard roof on a car. It allows the vehicle to become a convertible or open-top.

ONLINE RESOURCES

To learn more about Lamborghinis, please visit **abdobooklinks.com** or scan this QR code. These links are routinely monitored and updated to provide the most current information available.

INDEX